Those Amazing Alligators

Those Amazing Alligators

Kathy Feeney

Illustrated by Steve Weaver

Pineapple Press, Inc.
Sarasota, Florida

Inquiries should be addressed to:

Pineapple Press, Inc.
P.O. Box 3889
Sarasota, Florida 34230

www.pineapplepress.com

Library of Congress Cataloging-in-Publication Data

Feeney, Kathy, 1954-
Those amazing alligators / Kathy Feeney.-- 1st ed.
p. cm.
Includes bibliographical references (p.   ) and index.
ISBN-13: 978-1-56164-356-1 (pbk. : alk. paper)
ISBN-10: 1-56164-356-4 (pbk. : alk. paper)
ISBN-13: 978-1-56164-359-2
ISBN-10: 1-56164-359-9
1. Alligators--Juvenile literature.   I. Title.
QL666.C925F44 2006
597.98'4--dc22

2005030581

First Edition
Hb 10 9 8 7 6 5 4 3 2 1
Pb 10 9 8 7 6 5 4 3 2 1

Design by Steve Weaver
Printed in China

For RJ

Contents

What are alligators?

Alligators are large reptiles. They have tough scaly hides and huge lizard-shaped bodies. Alligators have four short legs with webbed feet. They have long flat tails. There are two species, or kinds, of alligators: the Chinese Alligator and the American Alligator. The Chinese Alligator lives in China. This book is about the American Alligator. Scientists call this species *Alligator mississippiensis*.

ALLIGATOR MISSISSPPIENSIS
ALIAS: GATOR, SWAMP LIZARD

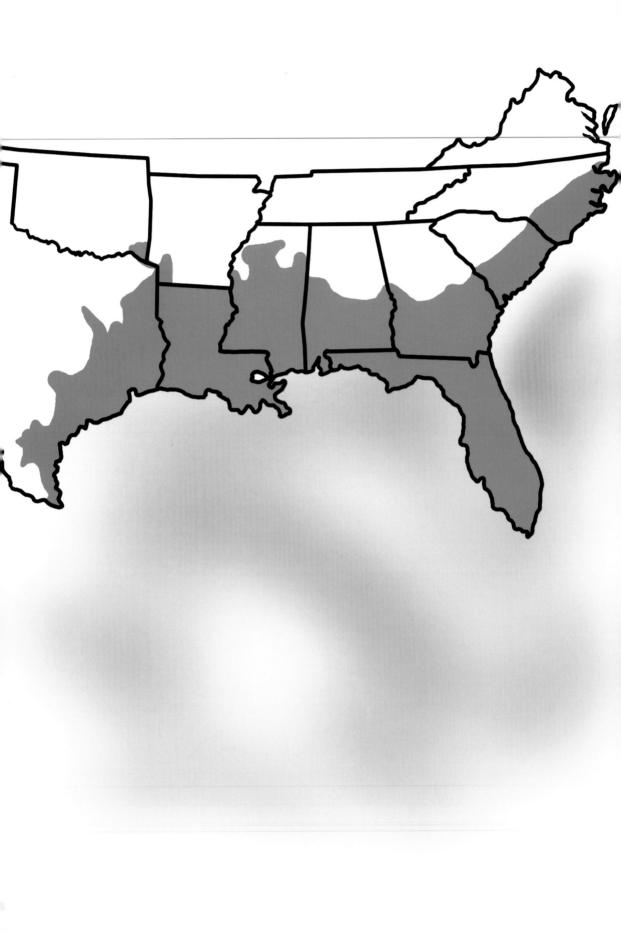

Where do alligators live in the wild?

Alligators live in the southeastern United States. They inhabit marshland, swamps, and rivers. They also live in canals, ponds, and lakes. Alligators live throughout Florida and Louisiana. They are also found in parts of Alabama, Arkansas, Georgia, Mississippi, North Carolina, Oklahoma, South Carolina, and Texas.

American
Alligator

American
Crocodile

What is the difference between an alligator and a crocodile?

Alligators and crocodiles are related. They belong to the scientific family called crocodilians. You can tell the difference between alligators and crocodiles by their snouts. Alligators have broad, rounded snouts. Crocodiles have long, narrow snouts.

The American Crocodile lives in south Florida and in countries around the Caribbean Sea. It lives in saltwater areas where alligators only occasionally visit.

How did the alligator get its name?

Spanish explorers named the alligator *el lagarto*. That means "the lizard" in Spanish. In English, the word became "aligarto," and then "alligator." Alligators are commonly called "gators."

How long have alligators roamed the earth?

Alligators are related to dinosaurs. The ancestors of alligators appeared on earth more than 200 million years ago, during the time of the dinosaurs. Alligators and dinosaurs belong to a family called archosaurs. The name of this group means "ruling reptiles."

Do alligators live alone or in groups?

Alligators can often be found together, swimming or sunning. Unlike other reptiles, young alligators stay with their mothers for up to two years. After the babies hatch from their eggs, the mother carefully moves them from the nest by carrying them in her mouth. The mother protects them from danger. Animals that eat baby alligators include birds, bobcats, otters, raccoons, and even adult alligators.

What do alligators eat?

Alligators are carnivores, or meat eaters. They hunt for food in and around water. Once the prey is killed and crunched up a bit in the big mouth, it is swallowed whole. Gulp! Young alligators eat frogs, insects, snails, crabs, shrimp, and tadpoles. Adult alligators eat just about any animal, including frogs, fish, turtles, snakes, birds, and mammals. When the gator is full, it may take the rest of its meal and store it in its gator hole or hide it along the bank.

When it gets hungry again, the alligator comes back for the rest of its food.

How many teeth do alligators have?

Alligators have about 80 teeth. The babies have sharp teeth. Adult gators have big strong teeth that can hold onto prey. Their powerful jaws can crush turtle shells and animal bones. When alligators lose, damage, or wear down their teeth, new ones grow in.

According to herpetologists (scientists who study reptiles), one alligator may grow as many as 3,000 replacement teeth during its lifetime.

How big are alligators?

Baby alligators weigh approximately two ounces when they hatch. That is about the weight of a tennis ball. Baby alligators are about eight inches long. They grow one foot each year. Adult female alligators weigh up to 300 pounds and grow to 8 or 9 feet long. Scientists say that some adult males have grown up to 18 feet long. That is about the length of a canoe. A few old males may weigh close to 1,000 pounds!

Approximately half the length of an alligator is its tail. Alligators swim by pushing the water side to side with their strong, flat tails.

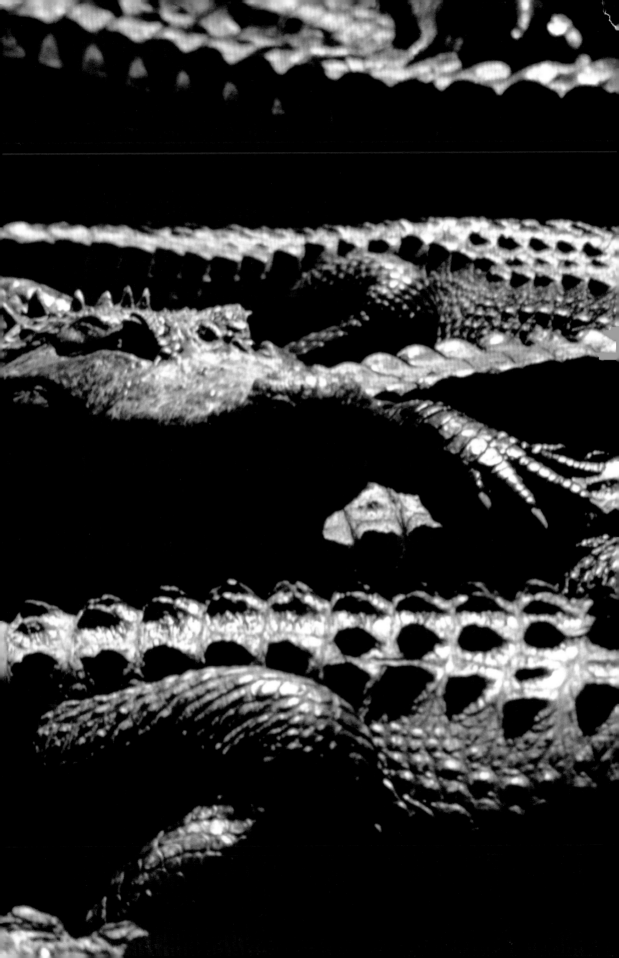

Why do alligators have bumps?

Alligators have rows of bony bumps on their backs and tails. They look like thick scaly spikes. Each bump is the outside cover of a piece of bone underneath an alligator's hide. They provide some protection, but their main purpose is to help the alligator increase its body temperature. Alligators are "cold-blooded," which means their bodies are the same temperature as their surroundings. So the alligator goes into the sun on cold days to warm up its body. If it's too hot, it goes into the water.

How do alligators communicate?

Alligators communicate with sounds and motions. In the spring a male alligator makes a sound like a roaring lion when it wants to attract a mate or when it wants to tell other males to stay away. Alligators snort, snap their jaws, and slam their heads against the surface of the water. Alligators can vibrate their bodies under water to make sounds only other alligators can hear.

How long do alligators live?

According to scientists, alligators in the wild can live from 35 to 50 years. Alligators living in captivity, at zoos and other places where people feed and take care of them, can live to be 60 to 80 years old. When an alligator is about four years old, it is big enough to escape danger and its chances of living a long life increase.

What color are an alligator's eyes?

Alligators have yellow-brown eyes with black pupils. At night, when light shines on the eyes of an alligator, they usually appear ruby red. Alligators have excellent eyesight. Their eyes, ears, and nostrils are on the top of their heads so they can see, hear, and breathe as they swim near the surface. This allows them to sneak up on their prey.

How fast can an alligator run?

Alligators have extremely short legs. They have five toes on their front legs and four webbed toes on their back legs. Alligators travel by swimming and walking. But they can also run. Some scientists say alligators can run 30 miles per hour over short distances of up to 100 feet. That is about as fast as an Olympic speed skater! Alligators can walk for miles if they need to find food.

How many eggs does the female alligator lay?

A female alligator lays 20 to 60 eggs in a nest she has made from plants, sticks, and mud. As the nest begins to decay, or rot, it gives off heat and keeps the eggs warm. The eggs incubate in this muddy mound for at least 2 months. The temperature of the nest determines whether the alligators will be male or female. Cooler nests make female alligators. Males come from warmer nests. When the nests have temperatures that are in between, both males and females hatch.

What is an alligator's "egg tooth"?

A baby alligator has an "egg tooth" on top of its snout. The hatchling uses this short tooth to break out of its shell. Alligator babies make grunting sounds when they are ready to hatch. The cries alert their mother to scratch an opening in the nest so the hatchlings can come out. Then the mother carries the newborn alligators in her mouth to the water.

Why do baby alligators have stripes?

Adult alligators have dark gray or black hides with small spikes across their backs and tails. They have cream-colored bellies. Baby alligators are black with bright yellow spots and stripes. This coloring camouflages, or hides, the babies to keep them safe. The stripes on baby alligators look like the leaves and grasses where they live.

Are alligators endangered?

In 1973, alligators were on the endangered species list. "Endangered species" are animals in danger of becoming extinct, or disappearing forever. Now alligators are no longer endangered, but they are still protected so they can live in the wild. Do not swim or walk near alligators. The best thing we can do is to leave wild alligators alone.

What is a white alligator?

White alligators are rare. They look like other alligators, except for their white hides and blue eyes. They are born without color cells in their skin. Some people say the white alligator looks like white chocolate. White alligators do not blend into their surroundings and are in danger of being eaten when they are babies. They are also in danger of being badly sunburned.

You can see white alligators in the Louisiana Swamp Exhibit at the Audubon Zoo in New Orleans and a few other alligator exhibits.

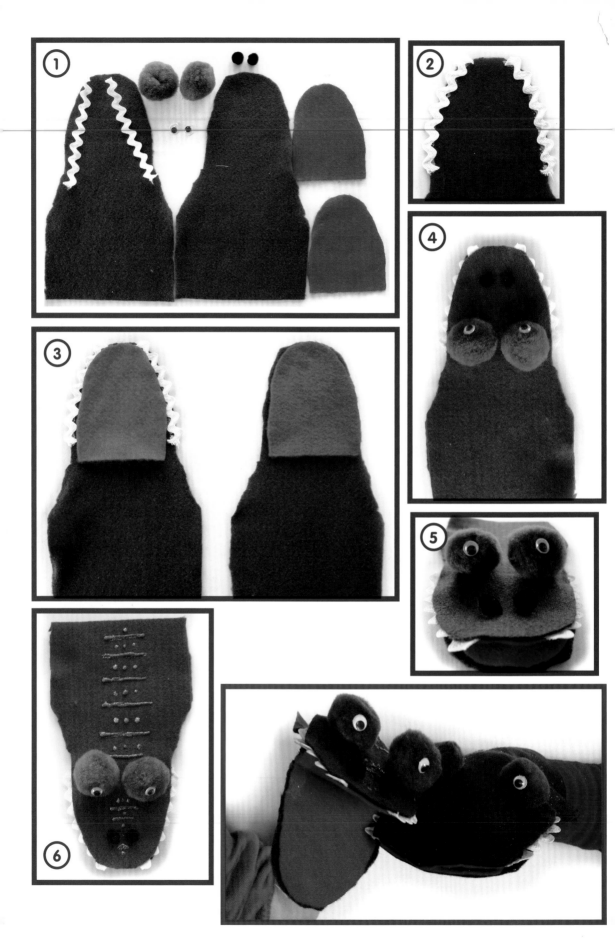

Make a Glitter Gator Puppet

Materials:

Two pieces of green felt
Two pieces of red felt
Two large green pompoms
Two small black pompoms

Two wiggle eyes
White rickrack
Scissors
Glue
Green glitter glue pen

1. Cut two pieces for the top and bottom of the gator from the green felt, making sure they are big enough to fit your hand, as shown in figure 1.
2. Cut two rounded pieces from the red felt for the insides of the gator's mouth. Make them just a little bit smaller than the snout part of the green felt pieces, as shown in figure 1.
3. Glue rickrack under the top sides of one of the green snouts, as shown in figure 2.
4. Glue the edges of the red felt mouth insides to the edges of the green snouts, leaving openings at the back for your hand, as shown in figure 3.
5. Glue the edges of the back half of the top and bottom of the gator together, as shown in figure 4.
6. Glue two green pompoms on the top for the eyes. Glue wiggle eyes to the pompoms, as shown in figure 5.
7. Glue two small black pompoms to the front of the snout for the nostrils, as shown in figure 5.
8. Create scales for your alligator with a glitter gel pen, as shown in figure 6.
9. Let your gator dry overnight.

If your friends make gator puppets too, you can have gator "conversations" and even gator puppet shows.

Make an Alligator Clothespin Magnet
Materials:

Glue
One piece of green felt
Small flat magnet

Scissors
One clothespin
Two tiny wiggle eyes

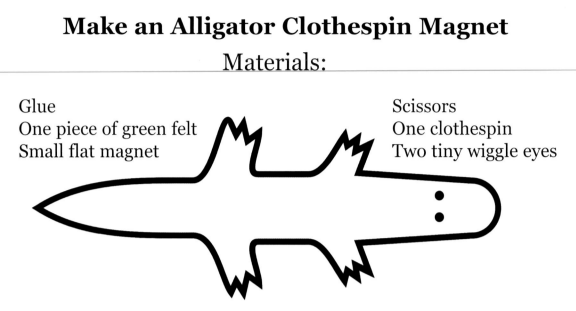

1. Make a photocopy of the alligator template (above).
2. Cut two alligators from the felt, using the template as your guide.
3. Glue one alligator to the top of the clothespin. Make sure that the head of the alligator is glued to the closed part of the clothespin. Then glue the other alligator to the bottom of the clothespin.
4. Glue wiggle eyes on the head of the gator.
5. Glue a magnet on the back of the gator clothespin.
6. Place a message in your alligator clothespin magnet and put it on the refrigerator!

Make an Alligator Bookmark

Materials:
Green construction paper
Scissors
Glue
Two wiggle eyes

1. Make a photocopy of the alligator bookmark (below).
2. Cut out your alligator bookmark from the green construction paper, using the template as your guide.
3. Glue wiggle eyes on both sides of the bookmark.
4. Place your bookmark in your favorite book!

Glossary

ancestors – ancient relatives

carnivore – a meat-eating animal

cold-blooded – describes an animal whose body is the same temperature as its surroundings

communicate – to share information, ideas, or feelings

endangered species – animals in danger of becoming extinct, or disappearing forever

hatch – to come from an egg

herpetologist – scientist who studies reptiles

hide – the skin of an animal

prey – an animal that is hunted for food

reptiles – cold-blooded animals that reproduce by laying eggs

Where to learn more about alligators

Some books about alligators:

Dennard, Deborah, and Jennifer Owings Dewey (Illustrator). *Alligators and Crocodiles (Our Wild World)*. Minnetonka, Minnesota: T&N Children's Publishing, 2003. (ages 7–10)

Richardson, Adele. *Alligators (Bridgestone Books World of Reptiles)*. Mankato, Minnesota: Capstone Press, 2005. (ages 9–12)

Rockwell, Ann F., and Lizzy Rockwell (Illustrator). *American Alligators (Let's-Read-and-Find-Out Science Books)*. New York, New York: HarperCollins Publishers, 2006. (ages 4–8)

Wexo, John Bonnett. *Alligators & Crocodiles (Zoo Books)*. Poway, California: Wildlife Education, Ltd., 2003. (all ages)

Some good alligator websites:

Florida Fish and Wildlife Conservation Commission
www.wildflorida.org/critters/alligators.asp

Nature Online (PBS)
www.pbs.org/wnet/nature/reptiles/gators_resources.html

Everglades National Park (Alligators)
www.nps.gov/ever/eco/gator.htm

Gatorland
www.gatorland.com/sitemap.html

St. Augustine Alligator Farm Zoological Park
www.alligatorfarm.com

World Almanac For Kids
www.worldalmanacforkids.com/explore/animals/alligator.html

About the Author

Kathy Feeney is the author of more than 26 books for children. She earned a degree in journalism from the University of South Florida in Tampa. Kathy lives in Tampa with her husband, RJ, and their two border terriers, Miss Muggle and Maxwell Smart. Alligators are among Kathy's favorite animals, as are koalas like the one she's holding in this photo (since it's hard to cuddle with an alligator!). You can visit her at www.KathyFeeney.com.

Index

If you enjoyed reading this book, here are some other Pineapple Press titles you might enjoy as well. To request our complete catalog or to place an order, write to Pineapple Press, P.O. Box 3889, Sarasota, Florida 34230, or call 1-800-PINEAPL (746-3275). Or visit our website at www.pineapplepress.com.

Those Outrageous Owls by Laura Wyatt. Illustrated by Steve Weaver, photographs by H. G. Moore III. Learn what owls eat, how they hunt, and why they look the way they do. You'll find out what an owlet looks like, why horned owls have horns, and much more! Ages 5–9.

Those Terrific Turtles by Sarah Cussen. Illustrated by Steve Weaver, photographs by David M. Dennis. This book of questions and answers will convince you that turtles are indeed terrific! You'll learn the difference between a turtle and a tortoise, and find out why they have shells. Meet baby turtles and some very, very old ones, and even explore a pond. Ages 5–9.

Those Excellent Eagles by Jan Lee Wicker. Illustrated by Steve Weaver, photographs by H.G. Moore III. Learn all about those excellent eagles—what they eat, how fast they fly, why the American Bald Eagle is our nation's national bird. You'll even make some edible eagles! Ages 5–9.

Those Peculiar Pelicans by Sarah Cussen. Illustrated by Steve Weaver, photographs by Roger Hammond. Find out how much food those peculiar pelicans can fit in their beaks, how they stay cool, whether they really steal fish from fishermen. And learn how to fold up an origami pelican. Ages 5–9.

Those Funny Flamingos by Jan Lee Wicker. Illustrated by Steve Weaver. Flamingos are indeed funny birds. Learn why those funny flamingos are pink, stand on one leg, eat upside down, and much more. Ages 5–9.

Drawing Florida Wildlife by Frank Lohan. The clearest, easiest method yet for learning to draw Florida's birds, reptiles, amphibians, and mammals. All ages.

Dinosaurs of the South by Judy Cutchins and Ginny Johnston. Dinosaurs lived in the southeastern United States. Loaded with full-color fossil photos as well as art to show what the dinos might have looked like. Ages 8–12.

Ice Age Giants of the South by Judy Cutchins and Ginny Johnston. Learn about the huge animals and reptiles that lived here during the Ice Age. Meet saber-toothed cats, dire wolves, mammoths, giant sloths, and more. Ages 8–12.

Giant Predators of the Ancient Seas by Judy Cutchins and Ginny Johnston. Meet the giant creatures that prowled the waters of prehistory. Ages 8–12.

Florida A to Z by Susan Jane Ryan. Illustrated by Carol Tornatore. From Alligator to Zephyrhills, you'll find out more about Florida packed in this alphabet than you can imagine—200 facts and pictures on Florida history, geography, nature, and people. Ages 8–12.

Florida Lighthouses for Kids by Elinor De Wire. Learn why some lighthouses are tall and some short, why a cat parachuted off St. Augustine Lighthouse, where Florida skeleton and spider lighthouses stand, and much more. Lots of color pictures. Ages 9 and up.